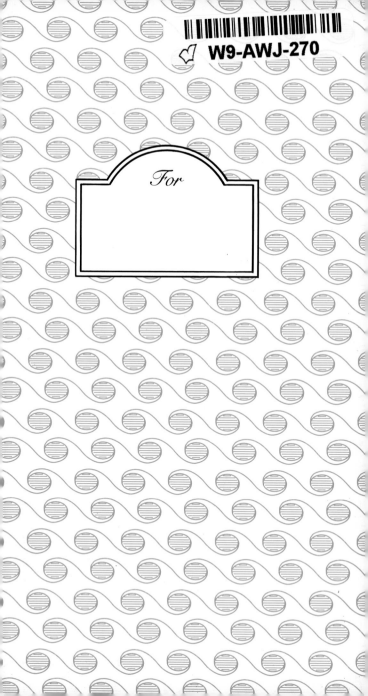

W9-AWJ-270

For

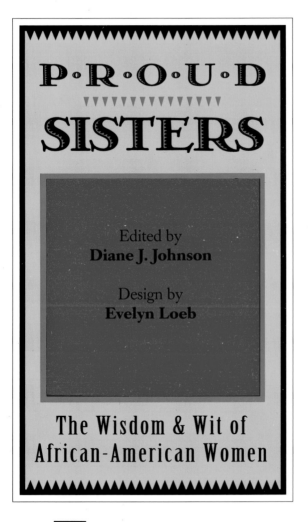

P·R·O·U·D
SISTERS

Edited by
Diane J. Johnson

Design by
Evelyn Loeb

The Wisdom & Wit of
African-American Women

PETER PAUPER PRESS, INC.
WHITE PLAINS, NEW YORK

For my mother, my twin sister Angela, my Aunt Gloria, my ancestry of Chisum and Johnson women, and my wonderful women colleagues and friends.

Photographs reprinted with the permission of FPG International: Mark Harmel photo p. 6; Ron Chapple photos pp. 11, 26, 32 and 50; Michael Krasowitz photo p. 14; Rob Lang photo p. 21; Ron Rovtar photo p. 38; and Frank Gordon photo p. 47. Page 54 photo courtesy of Ethel Mills.

Contents

Introduction

In this edition of quotations by women of African descent, Black women evidence in their own words their strength, creativity, passion, struggle, and down-to-earth wisdom and humor.

As I formulated this collection, I kept wondering why I had not before this project heard more about these phenomenal women. I discovered a history of African-American women writing poetry and prose since the 1770's, and I gained a greater appreciation for the thoughts of Maria W. Stewart, Zora Neale Hurston, Fanny Lou Hamer, June Jordan, Alice Walker, and many others. I felt, as had Marita Bonner, that:

> page after page put flesh and blood
> on the bones of the past. . . . This was
> all mine. This wealth. This panorama
> of genius and endurance.

This collection is an attempt to share that genius, endurance, intelligence, and light. It includes both famous and little-known women who tell what is meaningful to them, and what they think is essential in the grand scheme of things—in the expression of their creativity, in the search for love, in the delineation of justice, in the face of courage, and in the course of everyday life.

Hopefully, readers will find inspiration, humor, and much food for thought in these pages. These quotes, though only a snapshot of the way some women of African descent perceive and experience this complex, oft-times unjust, volatile, and exhilarating world, do reflect the laughter, the sorrow, the pain, the ferocity, the dignity, and the love of Black women.

As Susan L. Taylor has said:

> Words have the power to wound or to heal, to attract or repel, and [I must] think before I speak, weigh my words, because once spent they can't be retrieved.

D. J. J.

THE LEGACY OF
BEING BLACK

When I was a child, it did not occur to me,
even once, that the black in which I was
encased (I called it brown in those days)
would be considered, one day, beautiful.
Considered beautiful and called beautiful by
great groups.

GWENDOLYN BROOKS
Writer

The majestic splendor of the Black woman's
body . . . ebony magic that, after all is said
and done, never fails to keep us going in high
style!

BONNIE ALLEN
Fashion editor

The day I looked at myself with a natural was
the first time I liked what I saw.

MARITA GOLDEN
Writer

Black woman—the only legitimate *Cinderella* in modern America, complete with head rag, broom, and being left to make your own damned dress for a ball you'll have to crash.

GLORIA NAYLOR
Novelist

For years we've been hanging our maid's uniforms in the same closet as our tiaras and fox stoles. Black style is nothing if not inconsistent.

BONNIE ALLEN
Fashion editor

Because I and my reality did not comport with what they accepted as their reality, I and my reality had to be reconstructed by the Senate committee members with assistance from the press and others.

ANITA HILL
Law professor

When I cast my eyes on the long list of illustrious names that are enrolled on the bright annals of fame among the whites, I turn my eyes within, and ask my thoughts, "Where are the names of *our* illustrious ones?"

MARIA W. STEWART
Teacher, orator

Until 1967 my own blackness did not confront me with a shrill spelling of itself. I knew that I was what most people were calling "a Negro"; I called myself that, although always the word fell awkwardly on a poet's ear; I had never liked the sound of it.

GWENDOLYN BROOKS
Writer

I do not feel inhibited or bound by what I am. That does not mean that I have never had bad scenes relating to being Black and/or a woman, it means that other people's craziness has not managed to make me crazy.

LUCILLE CLIFTON
Writer

Every time I read *The Bluest Eye*, I weep for that little girl lost in a world of pain and for all the women who carry pieces and parts of that little girl buried somewhere in their spirits. For who among us has not at some point in time succumbed to the propaganda, looked in a mirror and felt ourselves to be wanting?

MARCIA ANN GILLESPIE
Editor

The special plight and the role of black women is not something that just happened three years ago. We've had a special plight for 350 years. My grandmother had it. My grandmother was a slave.

FANNIE LOU HAMER
Activist

Black people have been traumatized and psychically wounded. This is something we cannot discuss enough at this historical moment.

BELL HOOKS
Activist, sociologist

But I am not tragically colored. There is no great sorrow dammed up in my soul, nor lurking behind my eyes. I do not mind at all. I do not belong to the sobbing school of Negrohood who hold that nature somehow has given them a lowdown dirty deal and whose feelings are hurt about it. . . . No, I do not weep at the world–I am too busy sharpening my oyster knife.

ZORA NEALE HURSTON
Writer, cultural anthropologist

Until my singing made me famous, I'd lived so far inside the colored people's world that I didn't have to pay attention every day to the way some white people in this country act toward a person with a darker skin.

MAHALIA JACKSON
Singer

To be Black and marginally comfortable, I have to accept a gradual change of the oppressive status quo; act dumb enough not to threaten white people, but appear intelligent enough to be useful and worthy of their liberal investment . . .

JUDY SIMMONS
Journalist

When I was in the third grade I wanted to be
president. I can still remember the stricken
look on my teacher's face when I announced
it in class. By the time I was in the fourth
grade I had decided to be the president's wife
instead. It never occurred to me that I could
be neither because I was Black.

MICHELE WALLACE
Feminist, writer

You must understand, being Black is more
involved than just wearing an X cap. It means
being committed to furthering our race and
nurturing our children. Being Black runs
deeper than just having rhythm. It means
possessing a history of more than 300 years
of fighting for freedom and equality.

ELIZABETH RIDLEY
Teacher

My skin color causes certain problems con-
tinuously, problems which open the issue of
racism over and over, like a wound. These
openings are occasions for reexamination. My
skin color keeps things, literally, from being
either black or white.

TOI DERRICOTTE
Writer

INSPIRATION, CREATIVITY, AND ART

In my world, black women can do anything.

JULIE DASH
Filmmaker

Whatever good I have accomplished as an actress I believe came in direct proportion to my efforts to portray black women who have made positive contributions to my heritage.

CICELY TYSON
Actress

Singing is not a luxury, it is a requirement.

BERNICE JOHNSON REAGON
A cappella singer, cultural anthropologist,
founder of Sweet Honey in the Rock

[In my book, *Fearless Beadwork,*] I get to do things I would never do in real life, like be a superhero, wear high heels and spandex. And see how kinky hair acts when it's flying in the wind.

JOYCE SCOTT
Beadwork artist

I don't feel that I opened the door. I've never been a great mover and shaker of the earth. I think that those who came after me deserve a great deal of credit for what they have achieved. I don't feel that I am responsible for any of it, because if they didn't have it in them, they wouldn't be able to get it out.

MARIAN ANDERSON
Singer

Singing is my way of opening my arms and heart and letting what's in me come out.

JENNY BURTON
Singer

I have not written my experiences in order to attract attention to myself; on the contrary, it would have been more pleasant to me to have been silent about my own history. . . . But I do earnestly desire to arouse the women of the North to a realizing sense of the condition of two millions of women at the South, still in bondage, suffering what I suffered and most of them far worse.

HARRIET JACOBS
Former slave

I am an ordinary human being who is impelled to write poetry. . . . I still do feel that a poet has a duty to words, and that words can do wonderful things, and it's too bad to just let them lie there without doing anything with and for them.

GWENDOLYN BROOKS
Writer

The narratives . . . that kept me company, along with the living, breathing people in my life, were those that talked honestly about growing up black in America. They burst into my silence, and in my head, they shouted and chattered and whispered and sang together. I am writing . . . to become part of that unruly conversation, and to bring my experience back to the community of minds that made it possible.

LORENE CARY
Writer

I continue to create because writing is a labor of love and also an act of defiance, a way to light a candle in a gale wind.

ALICE CHILDRESS
Playwright, actress

I'd just like to have good work that I can be proud of and hope that I've crossed the color line and opened doors for others who come behind me.

HALLE BERRY
Actress

I consider myself a spokesperson for women all over America, all over the world because no matter what color you are, every woman has experienced what I'm singing about.

TONI BRAXTON
Singer

Each person has a literature inside them. But when people lose language, when they have to experiment with putting their thoughts together on the spot–that's what I love most. That's where character lives.

ANNA DEAVERE SMITH
Actress

I try never to take myself for granted as somebody who should be out there speaking. Rather, I'm doing it only because I feel there's something important that needs to be conveyed.

ANGELA DAVIS
Activist

I have come to believe over and over again that what is most important to me must be spoken, made verbal and shared, even at the risk of having it bruised or misunderstood. That the speaking profits me, beyond any other effect.

AUDRE LORDE
Poet, activist, writer

I had, I felt, more pressing and interesting things to do, such as reading and studying the history and literature of black women, a history that had been totally ignored, a contemporary literature bursting with originality, passion, insight and beauty.

BARBARA CHRISTIAN
Sociologist, writer, college professor

I learned [in beauty pageants] to be a good winner—and a good loser. Which helps my acting; every day I face rejection.

HALLE BERRY
Actress

Dance can free people from some of their oppressions. Just by using the body in its rhythmic patterns, it heightens circulation. Then if you work hard enough . . . there is a purifying process in dancing.

KATHERINE DUNHAM
Choreographer, dancer

I think art can be a wonderful way to affirm self. . . . Often what we write, the music we write, and the pictures we paint are dialogues with our deepest consciousness.

MARITA GOLDEN
Writer

This is one of the glories of man, the inventiveness of the human mind and the human spirit: whenever life doesn't seem to give an answer, we create one.

LORRAINE HANSBERRY
Writer, playwright

For women, then, poetry is not a luxury. It is a vital necessity of our existence. It forms the quality of the light within which we predicate our hopes and dreams toward survival and change, first made into language, then into idea, then into more tangible action. Poetry is the way we help give name to the nameless so it can be thought. The farthest horizons of our hopes and fears are cobbled by our poems, carved from the rock experiences of our daily lives.

AUDRE LORDE
Poet, activist, writer

From the very beginning, I saw myself as writing ... for those who would care about ... women not only because of their unique individualities, but also because of what they represent: black women/writers struggling against unfavorable odds to create their personal and artistic selves.

GLORIA T. HULL
Sociologist, women studies researcher

Good poetry and successful revolution change our lives. And you cannot compose a good poem or wage a revolution without changing consciousness. And you cannot alter consciousness unless you attack the language that you share with your enemies and invent a language that you share with your allies.

JUNE JORDAN
Poet, essayist

Your cultural center, the lifestyle of your people, is the most important single mechanism in your life, and you must be in control of it at all times. My concept of me is who I am.

ELMA LEWIS
Arts activist

[My mother] sees herself, her family history, her culture, her experiences, as dimensions of her craft, and she asks the same of others . . .

SARAH LAWRENCE-LIGHTFOOT
Sociologist

The affirmation that has come to me from individuals and locations that are on the margins strengthens and inspires me.

BELL HOOKS
Activist, sociologist

A writer does not always write in the ways others wish. . . . I am giving myself permission to write books that do not depend on anyone's liking them, because what I want to do is write better.

TONI MORRISON
Pulitzer prize-winning author

My changes taught me that words have the power to wound or to heal, to attract or to repel, and that I best think before I speak, weigh my words, because once spent they can't be retrieved.

SUSAN L. TAYLOR
Editor

My goal is to find ways to portray women in important roles–to help us feel more positive about ourselves.

PETRONIA PALEY
Actress

I need to keep thinking and analyzing, and have that transformed onto a piece of paper. Besides, if we as African-American women don't write our own books, then other folks will continue to define us.

JOHNNETTA B. COLE
President, Spelman College

Imagination! who can sing thy force?
Or who describe the swiftness of thy
　　　course?
Soaring through air to find the bright
　　　abode . . .

PHILLIS WHEATLEY
Poet (1773)

LOVE

I love myself when I am laughing.
And then again when I am looking mean and impressive.

ZORA NEALE HURSTON
Writer, cultural anthropologist

While I know myself as a creation of God, I am also obligated to realize and remember that everyone else and everything else are also God's creation.

MAYA ANGELOU
Poet, writer

I had journeyed, tamed the wild terrain of my dreams. Had become a Black woman citing a new beginning every day. Discovery. Anger. All made me the woman they told my mother she could never be. But was. Inside. Didn't know it. Cringed at the thought. I mined the dream. Pride was the treasure. Wiping blood from the lid, cautious hand lifting, looked inside. Saw the self always there. Affirmed. Made whole. Free.

MARITA GOLDEN
Writer

You'll never get a boy friend if you don't stop reading those books.

GWENDOLYN BROOKS
Writer
Maud Martha

I don't believe that life is supposed to make you feel good, or to make you feel miserable either. Life is just supposed to make you feel.

GLORIA NAYLOR
Novelist

Often I was in some lonesome wilderness, suffering strange things and agonies . . . cosmic loneliness was my shadow. Nothing and nobody around me really touched me. It is one of the blessings of this world that few people see visions and dream dreams.

ZORA NEALE HURSTON
Writer, cultural anthropologist

People are seldom loved because they have a perfect nose. When a man tells me I'm beautiful, I enjoy it. Then I wait for him to say, "And you're so intelligent. . . ."

BARBARA HENDRICKS
Opera singer

One of the nicest realizations that I've come
to over the past two years is that I'm finally
learning to love all of my selves.

WISTA JOHNSON
Editor

I would like to be finished with shame, to
know I love myself and my own people, that
I believe I have something positive to con-
tribute . . .

TOI DERRICOTTE
Writer

Black women know it's impossible to cuddle
up to a piece of steel. And granite is no place
to nestle! Many a black man has frankly
declared that life is too trying for him to
come home and face a tough woman . . .

JEANNE NOBLE
Writer

I want to stop being my own worst enemy
and start being my best friend. I want to
decide who I am, mostly, and what work I
want to do, seriously.

JUDY SIMMONS
Journalist

Who can tell the bitter anguish
Of a true and noble heart?
Who can quote in simple language
Words which bid its grief depart?
When its dearest earthly treasure,
When its life, its love, its all,
He who ever sought its pleasure
From earth to heaven is called.

ANNA BELLE RHODES PENN
Poet
Grief Unknown (1834)

O my people, my people. We be word wiz-
ards. . . . Ask, "You love me?" and we might
answer, "Do birds fly?. . . Is coal black?" Or, if
the feeling is unrequited, we might say, "I
wouldn't give up air if you was stopped up in
a jug."

VERTAMAE SMART-GROSVENOR
Radio journalist, writer

Love is like a favorite pen. You'll write with it,
you'll show it off and you won't let anyone
else use it. But when it runs out of ink, sometimes it's hard to find a refill.

LATOYA SMITH
Student

There are these official religious edicts, and then there are the very private, painful decisions people make to make their lives livable. All my work is about intimacy–God in all those places of intimacy and pain and contradiction. So I'm trying to whisper into the ears of my sisters, who may be living something different from what has been officially mandated. And say, "It's all right."

RENITA WEEMS
Divinity school professor

Loves music. Loves dance. Loves the moon. *Loves* the Spirit. Loves love and food and roundness. Loves struggle. *Loves* the Folk. Loves herself. *Regardless.*

ALICE WALKER
Writer

FAMILY AND OUR HERITAGE

I don't believe that the accident of birth makes people sisters or brothers. It makes them siblings. Gives them mutuality of parentage. Sisterhood and brotherhood is a condition people have to work at.

MAYA ANGELOU
Poet, writer

My parents were always philosophizing about how to bring about change. To me, people who didn't try to make the world a better place were strange.

CAROL MOSELEY BRAUN
U. S. Senator

If you are a parent, recognize that it is the most important calling and rewarding challenge you have. What you do every day, what you say and how you act, will do more to shape the future of America than any other factor.

MARIAN WRIGHT EDELMAN
Children's Defense Fund President

I thank God for strong, black men who are good fathers regardless of what else they are not, and whose love for their children is their faith in a brighter tomorrow.

BEBE MOORE CAMPBELL
Writer

. . . Things like that gave me my first glimmering of the universal female gospel that all good traits and leanings come from the mother's side.

ZORA NEALE HURSTON
Writer, cultural anthropologist

All my growth and development led me to believe that if you really do the right thing, and if you play by the rules, and if you got enough good, solid judgment and common sense, that you're going to be able to do whatever you want to do with your life. My father taught me that.

BARBARA JORDAN
College professor, former Congresswoman

As I watch my mother from the audience, I can feel the peacefulness that she emanates . . . She feels the confidence to speak . . . because she has a message they need to hear, and because she inherited eloquence and authority from her father . . .

SARAH LAWRENCE-LIGHTFOOT
Sociologist

I'm not afraid of too many things, and I got that invincible kind of attitude from [my father].

QUEEN LATIFAH
Rap singer, actress

Guided by my heritage of a love of beauty and a respect for strength–in search of my mother's garden I found my own.

ALICE WALKER
Writer

It is rare, I think, for parents to let their children–of any age–grow up and become peers.

SARAH LAWRENCE-LIGHTFOOT
Sociologist

I had formed the conviction that as soon as I could get a man, any man, to assume responsibility for me, I would no longer have to answer to my mother.

MICHELE WALLACE
Feminist, writer

When the emphasis shifted to blackness, to exploring and exalting the experience of blacks in the ghettos, we knew we were certainly not what anyone meant when they said that blacks were beautiful. We either had to get in on the black experience immediately or forever be confined to that purgatorylike state between black and white that was being middle-class and black.

MICHELE WALLACE
Feminist, writer

[My grandmother is] an ancestor figure, . . . –African and New World–who made my being possible, and whose spirit I believe continues to animate my life and work. I am, in a word, an unabashed ancestor worshipper.

PAULE MARSHALL
Novelist

I can't help having a political life. And I guess this is related to my background, growing up in the South where to be Black was to be political.

ANGELA DAVIS
Activist

When I envision the future, I think of the world I crave for my daughters and my sons. It is thinking for survival of the species–thinking for life.

AUDRE LORDE
Poet, activist, writer

If we want to be whole, we must recall the past, those parts that we want to remember, those parts that we want to forget.

BARBARA CHRISTIAN
Sociologist, writer, college professor

LIFE AND BEING A WOMAN

Am I not a Woman and a Sister?

L. H.
Former slave (1832)

We all have different backgrounds, but it is as if we are all part of the same sisterhood.

KIMBERLY CLARICE AIKEN
Miss America 1994

Life is what your creator gave you for free. Style is what you do with it.

DR. MAE C. JEMISON
Astronaut

Working is my life.

AILEEN HERNANDEZ
Public official, activist

Sometimes I act like a bitch for the same reasons that Sojourner Truth ripped off her bodice in public and asked, "Ain't I a woman too?" I mean, really, am I not somebody's child?

JUDY SIMMONS
Journalist

I make my own decisions and couldn't imagine anyone else doing that, because I'm in control of my own destiny. And if anything happens, or if a mistake is ever made, it's because it's something I chose to do . . .

JANET JACKSON
Entertainer

We are the one race of women who could offer such seemingly disparate styles as Rosa Parks' and Billie Holiday's as perfect examples of who we are, and find a little bit of them in each of us.

BONNIE ALLEN
Fashion editor

Deal with yourself as an individual worthy of respect and make everyone else deal with you the same way.

NIKKI GIOVANNI
Poet, activist

Some people who exist sparingly on the mean side of the hill are threatened by those who also live in the shadows but who celebrate the light.

MAYA ANGELOU
Poet, writer

People who get concerned about "feminocracy," who say diversity and inclusiveness are going too far, I don't subscribe to any of that.

SHARON SAYLES BELTON
Mayor of Minneapolis

When you are kind to someone in trouble, you hope they'll remember and be kind to someone else. And, it'll become like a wildfire.

WHOOPI GOLDBERG
Actress

I'm willing to take a chance because I really believe I'm going to win. But you're not going to win unless you try. You know, there was a time I was a picketer across the street. Then I decided I didn't want to be there outside of policy-making. I wanted to be inside, fighting right there on their turf.

YVONNE BRATHWAITE BURKE
Attorney, former Congresswoman

Now when you say, "We don't know *what* we'd do without her" this is a polite lie . . . because I know that if I dropped dead or had a stroke, you would get somebody to replace me.

ALICE CHILDRESS
Playwright, actress

Instead of wallowing in my misery, I just made some changes.

STEPHANIE MILLS
Actress

It is the responsibility of every adult–especially parents, educators, and religious leaders–to make sure that children hear what we have learned from the lessons of life and to hear over and over that we love them and that they are not alone.

MARIAN WRIGHT EDELMAN
Children's Defense Fund President

Tragedy is a part of living. Its random unfairness forces us to question who we are, what we are doing with our lives and even if life is worth it.

VANESSA J. GALLMAN
Journalist

When I was a child, my uncontrollable fine and curly hair would work its way out of braids, pigtails, and bobby pins, casting its fate to the wind. My mother would insist that I wear bangs, saying my forehead was too prominent. My hair was like my grandfather said my brothers and I were–weeds, without direction.

QUO VADIS GEX-BREAUX
Writer

Where there is a woman there is magic. If there is a moon falling from her mouth, she is a woman who knows her magic, who can share or not share her powers. A woman with a moon falling from her mouth, roses between her legs and tiaras of Spanish moss, this woman is a consort of the spirits.

NTOZAKE SHANGE
Author
Sassafrass, Cypress & Indigo

[She] saw her life like a great tree in leaf with the things suffered, things enjoyed, things done and undone. Dawn and doom was in the branches.

ZORA NEALE HURSTON
Writer, cultural anthropologist
Their Eyes Were Watching God

I care. I care about it all. It takes too much energy *not* to care. Yesterday I counted twenty-six gray hairs on the top of my head all from trying not to care. . . .

LORRAINE HANSBERRY
Writer, playwright
To Be Young, Gifted and Black

I have always been too old. I was taken out of kindergarten after only a day and put into first grade because my sixth birthday was due in a month. Even back then I was too old for the carefree first school days of playing, finger painting, naps and milk and cookies. I was thrown right into the hard-core addition and take-away and *Fun With Dick and Jane.*

CARLA A. MIKELL
TV production associate

When I was younger, there were things I was just too afraid to try. The really important thing as you get older is that you can do anything you want to.

MARY HELEN WASHINGTON
Editor, college professor

As I approach the middle years and beyond, I intend to remain interested (and interesting!), fit, curious, aware, progressive, flexible. I will continue to write about the things I dislike and the things I love. I'll never stop challenging life or growing and savoring it in all its mysteries and complexities.

KATHRYN IRVIN
Teacher, writer, poet

Hadn't the passage of four decades brought me, if not wisdom, at least a certain composure, authority and self-assurance? Couldn't time be considered an ally as well as an enemy?

PEGGY TAYLOR
Writer

My basic attitude is that you're only as old as you think you are. . . . I feel I have a lot of life in me.

ANNETTE SAMUELS
Press secretary

My biting sarcasm and shrill hysteria can make mincemeat of any man who looks as if he's about to trifle with my feelings, abandon me like my daddy did or break my heart.

LaDONNA MASON
Journalist

Black women want to be involved. They demand to be involved. Black women want to be partners, allies, sisters! Before there is partnering and sharing with someone, however, there is the becoming of oneself.

JEANNE NOBLE
Writer

Writing travels so much farther than you could ever go. Something that was part of me gets to go places that I may never see.

BARBARA SMITH
Book publisher, sociologist

I think back to the fifties when women were brought up to be nice. Obviously I grew up in the seventies, and what I'm trying to instill in my daughters is that you don't have to be nice all the time. . . . You don't have to listen to what others tell you just because they're older, or because they're boys.

VANESSA WILLIAMS
Former Miss America, entertainer

I'm in no hurry. In spite of all the worldly pressure for me to have a wedding, I no longer feel what I felt many years ago—that I have to have a man in order to make myself whole.

OPRAH WINFREY
TV personality

Every drop of water stains the silk but it doesn't destroy it. It marks it. Every negative imprint I absorbed during the months before I was official and certificated remains. You see my efforts to become began long before my date of birth.

GWENDOLYN J. DUNGY
Writer

Nobody really wants to be normal; it's just a defense mechanism.

DANITRA VANCE
Comedienne

For each of us as women, there is a dark place within, where hidden and growing our true spirit rises . . .

AUDRE LORDE
Poet, activist, writer

You cannot belong to anyone else, until you belong to yourself.

PEARL BAILEY
Singer

KNOWLEDGE AND LEARNING

One thing that never ceases to amaze me, along with the growth of vegetation from the earth and of hair from the head, is the growth of understanding.

ALICE WALKER
Writer

For one thing we can teach each other the differences in our experiences rather than struggling all the time to say, "It's the same." We can ask each other, "What's different about us?"

ALICE CHILDRESS
Playwright, actress

Human beings are more alike than unalike, and what is true anywhere is true everywhere, yet I encourage travel to as many destinations as possible for the sake of education as well as pleasure.

MAYA ANGELOU
Poet, writer

I wondered if they knew, or if they would learn, that just as St. Paul's was theirs, because they had attended the school and contributed to it, so, too, was American life and culture theirs, because they were black people in America.

LORENE CARY
Writer

Learning early on that good grades were rewarded while independent thinking was regarded with suspicion, I knew that it was important to be "smart" but not "too smart."

BELL HOOKS
Activist, sociologist

You know what my mother told me one day? I was feeling really good about some project I had finished, and she just sort of looked at me and said, "But you're illiterate." I was crushed. How could my mother consider me illiterate?

DR. MAE C. JEMISON
Astronaut

But you know that things learned need testing–acid testing–to see if they are really after all, an interwoven part of you.

MARITA BONNER
Writer

At my college [Smith], I felt a contentment that is hard to come by, one largely based on the assumption that a woman is not worth less than a man, that she is as likely to do great things (or not do them, if she so chooses) as a man. Developing ourselves as women is worth the effort–that was the lesson. Unfortunately it is one that many women never learn.

MARTHA SOUTHGATE
Writer

There is a *knowingness* that is as much a part of us as flesh and blood and bones. It's intuition, the deepest natural knowing. . . . Intuition is the voice within forever pressing us to stretch ourselves, to take risks, to keep loving and giving birth to a new self, regardless of circumstances.

SUSAN L. TAYLOR
Editor

COURAGE, RESISTANCE, AND STRUGGLE

The story of slavery never has been and never will be fully told. . . . It is because American slavery was "the vilest that ever saw the sun," that it is, and will remain forever, impossible to adequately portray its unspeakable horrors, its heart-breaking sorrows, its fathomless miseries of hopeless grief, its intolerable shames, and its heaven-defying and outrageous brutalities.

OCTAVIA V. R. ALBERT
19th-Century minister's wife

Knowledge is power.

OPRAH WINFREY
TV personality

Public policy is better when the people it's designed to affect are making it—especially women, the poor, and people of color.

SHARON SAYLES BELTON
Mayor of Minneapolis

There was only one place to finish and the place was Broadway. . . . I've been a working woman since I was 16, and after what I've been through–well, you get into a habit of surviving.

LENA HORNE
Actress, singer

America does not seem to remember that it derived its wealth, its values, its food, much of its medicine, and a large part of its "dream" from Native America.

PAULA GUNN ALLEN
Writer

This very place where I am now the mayor, the people used to arrest me every day and harass me every day. They turned cars upside down, burned crosses in my yard, threw homemade bombs at us. It wasn't just a song for us, "We Shall Overcome." It was our strength. When I see people heading up organizations and doing all these things, it didn't come about overnight and it didn't come without pain.

UNITA BLACKWELL
First black mayor in Mississippi

My mother viewed speaking impeccably proper English as a strategy in the overall battle for civil rights.

BEBE MOORE CAMPBELL
Writer

One must distinguish the desire for power from the need to become empowered–that is, seeing oneself as capable of and having the right to determine one's life.

BARBARA CHRISTIAN
Sociologist, writer, college professor

I have found that in the real sources are concealed my survival. My speech. My voice.

MICHELLE CLIFF
Writer

If you're talking about people without power, then essentially the only power you have is your combined energy, your combined visibility.

ANGELA DAVIS
Activist

I like to avoid confrontations if I can. But if I cannot, I want to be totally prepared to solve them or eliminate them, one way or another.

KATHERINE DUNHAM
Choreographer, dancer

There is no free lunch. Don't feel entitled to anything you don't sweat and struggle for.

MARIAN WRIGHT EDELMAN
Children's Defense Fund President

Never work just for money or for power. They won't save your soul or build a decent family or help you sleep at night.

MARIAN WRIGHT EDELMAN
Children's Defense Fund President

You know I work for the liberation of all people, because when I liberate myself, I'm liberating other people.

FANNIE LOU HAMER
Activist

I am ever mindful of the fact that the groups I belong to—African American people, women people—are still in the process of pulling the gags out of our mouths; that in speaking freely and publicly, in expressing our thoughts and feelings, we do so as much for our ancestors and foremothers as we do for ourselves.

MARCIA ANN GILLESPIE
Editor

As a country, we are in a state of denial about issues of race and racism. And too many of our leaders have concluded that the way to remedy racism is to simply stop talking about race.

LANI GUINIER
Asst. Atty. Gen. nominee, law professor

In everything we attempt, we must strive to welcome diversity rather than gather around us what is comforting and familiar.

ELIZABETH HIGGINBOTHAM
Writer, sociologist

I am a feminist, and what that means to me is much the same as the meaning of the fact that I am Black. It means that I must undertake to love myself and respect myself as though my very life depends upon self-love and self-respect.

JUNE JORDAN
Poet, essayist

The women's movement now has a strong flavor of an upper-class white women's movement. We have to move into the general society and get women to identify as feminists.

AILEEN HERNANDEZ
Public official, activist

How do we transform the meaninglessness that people feel into an effective form of struggle?

BELL HOOKS
Activist, sociologist

Am I my brother's keeper? I have to be. . . . We know and see the problems, because we *have* to live so close to them.

HELEN HOWARD
Writer

I am entering my soul in a struggle that will most certainly transform all the peoples of the earth: the movement into self-love, self-respect and self-determination is the movement now galvanizing the true majority of human beings everywhere.

JUNE JORDAN
Poet, essayist

Necessary social change reflects acts of caring among human beings. Participation in social change can result from the collaborative efforts of family and therapist.

MARGARET MORGAN LAWRENCE
Child psychoanalyst

While remaining unified as a people, we must diversify our energies . . . if progress is to continue. At the same time some Blacks are seeking political office, others must seek high office in the labor movement; prominent places in the corporate power structure; leadership among the American intelligentsia; and our appropriate places in American education, science, law, small business and the arts.

ELEANOR HOLMES NORTON
Public official, law professor

For those of you who are tired of hearing about racism, imagine how much more tired *we* are of constantly experiencing it, second by literal second, how much more exhausted we are to see it constantly in your eyes.

BARBARA SMITH
Book publisher, sociologist

I never learned much about what I need to be fulfilled skipping through life in my joy. Have you? My pain, my changes, have been the major source of my growth. We cut our teeth on our changes; they force us to expand and become the people we are meant to be.

SUSAN L. TAYLOR
Editor

I know a little mite 'bout Woman's Rights, too. I come forth to speak 'bout Woman's Rights, and want to throw in my little mite, to keep the scales a-movin. . . . We have all been thrown down so low that nobody thought we'd ever get up again; but we have been long enough trodden now; we will come up again, and now I am here.

SOJOURNER TRUTH
Anti-slavery activist (1832)

I looked at my hands to see if I was de same person now I was free. Dere was such a glory ober eberything, de sun came like gold trou de trees, and ober de fields, and I felt like I was in heaven.

HARRIET TUBMAN
Abolitionist

The riots in Los Angeles and in other cities shocked the world. They shouldn't have. Many of us have watched our country–including our government–neglect the problems, indeed the people, of our inner-cities for years–even as matters reached a crisis stage.

MAXINE WATERS
U.S. Congresswoman

Many South Africans, determined to vote even in the face of administrative and organizational obstacles, waited in line for 12 hours to exercise their hard-won right to full citizenship. Here in the U.S., where the threat of rain can keep thousands of citizens away from the polling stations, there is much to be learned from the South African election.

ELAINE R. JONES
*Director-Counsel, NAACP Legal Defense
and Educational Fund*

Is it any wonder our children have no hope?

MAXINE WATERS
U.S. Congresswoman

Some of my friends tell me I'm right on the edge of what white folks can take.

DANITRA VANCE
Comedienne

Every young person should be able to develop his or her potential in freedom and dignity.

RACHEL ROBINSON
Activist, widow of Jackie Robinson

I always say my God will take care of me. If it's my time I'll go, and if it's not I won't. I feel that He really has a lot of important things for me to do. And He's going to make sure that I'm here to do them.

JOYCELYN ELDERS
Surgeon General of the U.S.